First published in 1999 by Chancellor Press,
an imprint of Bounty Books,
a division of the Octopus Publishing Group Ltd
2–4 Heron Quays, London, E14 4JP

ISBN 0-75370-233-9

Created and Illustrated by
Charlie Anne Turner

Produced and Directed by
Linda Watters Book Packaging
2 Monklands Cottage,
Isle of Pins Road,
Troon, Ayrshire, KA10 7JS

Produced by Toppan (HK) Ltd
Printed in China

Rules For Cats

Created and Illustrated by
Charlie Anne Turner

CHANCELLOR PRESS

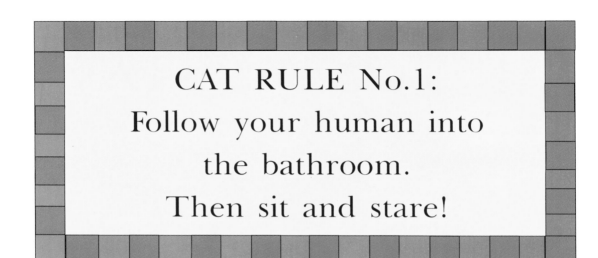

CAT RULE No.1:
Follow your human into
the bathroom.
Then sit and stare!

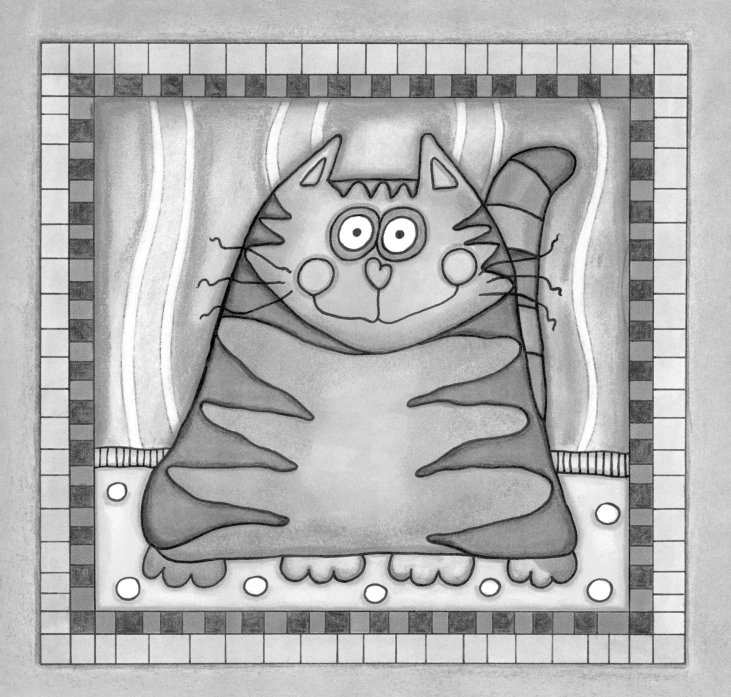

CAT RULE No.2:
Always remember to jump on your human's newspaper!

CAT RULE No.3:
Always be sick on the most
expensive rug, or just
behind bare feet!

CAT RULE No.4:
Repeatedly knock over ornaments that you don't like!

CAT RULE No.5:
Act as if you were starving at
all times - you will be fed!

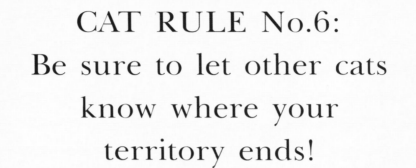

CAT RULE No.6:
Be sure to let other cats
know where your
territory ends!

CAT RULE No.7:
The best drinking water
is in the toilet bowl!

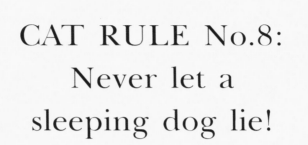

CAT RULE No.8:
Never let a
sleeping dog lie!

CAT RULE No.9:
Always stay close to
your human. They
will fall for you!

CAT RULE No.10:
You can make a
home anywhere!

CAT RULE No.11:
Bring your human a
present at least
once a week!

CAT RULE No.12:
Do not forget
to do your nails!

CAT RULE No.13:
Any form of exercise always
comes second to sleep!

CAT RULE No.14:
Never worry about
your weight!

CAT RULE No.15:
Bad breath is
to be cultivated!

CAT RULE No.16:
Encourage your human
not to buy you any
pink fluffy toys!

CAT RULE No.17:
If all else fails,
try sulking!

CAT RULE No.18:
Stay out late whenever
you like and never explain!

CAT RULE No.19:
Make sure your human sees
you reach those hard
to reach areas!

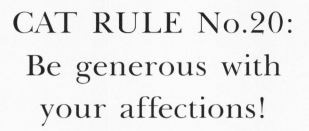

CAT RULE No.20:
Be generous with
your affections!